Measuring Cubits
While the
Thunder Claps

Measuring Cubits While the Thunder Claps

Poems by Gary J. Whitehead

David Robert Books

Published by David Robert Books
P.O. Box 541106
Cincinnati, OH 45254-1106

ISBN: 9781934999257
LCCN: 2008934848

Poetry Editor: Kevin Walzer
Business Editor: Lori Jareo

Visit us on the web at www.davidrobertbooks.com

Acknowledgments

Grateful acknowledgment is made to the following publications in which these poems first appeared:

Alimentum: "Almost Utopia"; "Plums"
Arabesques Review: "Recollection on What Would Have
    Been Our Anniversary"
Barrelhouse: "The Gaze"
The Blue Fifth: "The Infidel"
Chaffin Journal: "Double Sonnet"
Dogwood: "Canning Tomatoes"
English Journal: "Seven Hummingbirds"
Freshwater: "Jays Raving at Dawn"
High Desert Journal: "One Day in July"
Measure: "Rubaiyat for Chanterelles"
Poetry: "The Experiment"; "First Year Teacher to His
    Students"
The Providence Journal: "Pawtucket, Rhode Island: An
    Interment"
Right Hand Pointing: "Autumn in July"; "Prayer"
Smartish Pace: "A Mouse in the House"; "Total Lunar
    Eclipse"
Southern Poetry Review: "Falmouth"
West Wind Review: "Kindling"; "Sheep's Skull"

My special gratitude to PEN Northwest; to the Tenafly Board
of Education; and to Bradley, Frank and Margery Boyden for
my six-month residency at the Dutch Henry Homestead in
Oregon, where most of this book was written.

Some of these poems were previously published in the
chapbook *After the Drowning* (Finishing Line Press, 2006).
"Conch" appeared in the anthology *Salmon: A Journey in
Poetry,* Salmon Publishing, Ireland. "Monument" appeared in
Poem, Revised, Marion Street Press.

Grateful acknowledgment is also made to the following
organizations for their generous support:

Achill Heinrich Böll Committee, Ireland
Blue Mountain Center, Blue Mountain Lake, New York
Fine Arts Work Center, Provincetown, Massachusetts

The Geraldine R. Dodge Foundation, New Jersey
Mesa Refuge, Point Reyes, California
The New York Foundation for the Arts

for my mother and father

〜 〜 〜

Table of Contents

I.

A Used Book

—for Neil

When I open its pages my dog stirs
from his repose on the couch beside me
to sniff at the spine and trim. His gray ears
lift to listen, and I hear what he hears:
traffic horns, a teapot's whistle, the purrs
of the reader's cats on her old settee.

What was she doing reading such heady
stuff so early on a Saturday—sun
not yet risen, her lover still asleep?
The book, I guess, her company to keep,
and the cats, while the light kept its steady
course across her floor. Paris or London,

I imagine, though it was probably
San Francisco, a streetcar passing by
and fog rinsing the morning air. A gray
day then, much like any other. It may
be that she, too, drawn irresistibly
to its place on a shelf in a nearby

shop, blew the dust and bought it second-hand.
And perhaps her cats roused when she opened
its cover, catching the vague scent of dog,
and she got no further than the prologue
before she was off to some other land
where a man held a page against the wind.

One Day in July

All that I am
wrapped in a hammock's sway

and time sounded
in the small turnings of sprinklers

and fat flies.
Green gone brown. Road dust

asleep for the least
wind or any cloud's offering.

As easily as I lie here
I could die here for all that moves me,

grow bad as an apple
and fall in some patch of shade,

forgotten by all
I've forgotten and sweet as the legs of bees.

Out of this moment,
if ever I recall it, will rock the soft

pendulum of the human
I was, as naked and doomed and malcontent

as Adam still ribbed,
and mythic only to me. Who else

will remember
the bear I saw a few hours before

standing in a fir
like a logger, its breath like an engine,

or know another seven days
of silence and a single droning plane?

And if the same
could be said for every man alone

seeing the strange
and ordinary and storing them like seeds

for the tender shoots
of memory, passing time with little else

to grieve,
then it's no wonder God created Eve.

Recollection on What Would Have Been Our Anniversary

Her father had given us instruction—
tie back the awning if a hurricane
blew in—and she and I couldn't contain
               our grins. Destruction,

though, is every father's fear when he leaves
his girl alone. We offered our farewell
and wishes for godspeed to Portugal.
               Six days later the eaves

poured like tipped urns, and from her twin girlhood
bed I could see herring gulls tossed in gales
and leaves pulling like skeet from the maples.
               How in the world could

he have known? An almanac? A forecast?
But young love heeds neither warning nor proof.
We swirled tongues like clouds even as the roof's
               nails complained against

the pull. We rode our own salt swells. It took
the awning lashing the house to rouse us.
In less than a year we would be spouses.
               I climbed and unhooked

ropes from their moorings. I held on for life,
or tried to, as we tied the fabric fast.
For a time it held, like those years now past
               when I called her wife.

Plums

I like to slice them along the seam,
blade balanced on the fulcrum of pit
—that density, like bone, inside the flesh—
and roll until it's cut clean through.
Then the twist as if uncapping a jar,

and I'm holding hemispheres:
the center of one an oval cup, the other
an egg I pluck from its sweet nest.
But always before I eat each smooth half
comes the urge to put it all back together.

Full of Blood, and Irrelevant

If memory had fingers, it would wring
from me each forgettable day we shared.

The double-date drive to Plum Island
in the pouring rain, windows fogged

like shower glass. I'd listen now to your
every laugh. That Sunday morning,

March, repairing a botched crossword
while our clothes rolled in the laundromat's

mechanical song. What shirt were you
wearing? How long was your hair then?

A year in retrospect is a checked list
written in disappearing ink and clutched

in a tight fist. *Pick up shampoo. Take out
trash. Replace washer in kitchen sink.*

How many hours did we pass together?
Given the chance to do it over, would we

do it the same way? And if memory
did have fingers and those fingers formed

a fist, would our times shine out,
red as rubies, full of blood, and irrelevant?

Mouse in the House

For two nights now it's wakened me from dreams
with a sound like paper being torn, reams

of it, a scratching that's gone on for hours.
Blind in the dark, I think of my father's

letters, the ones composed but never sent.
They were addressed to his sister, my aunt,

a woman I never met but whose voice,
slurry and calling from some noisy place,

introduced itself one New Year's eve, late,
before my mother came and silenced it

with a click. She was one of many things
we never spoke of. But when the phone rang

at odd hours, I'd wonder if it was her.
That voice had resurrected the picture

in the silver frame, my parents' wedding
day: on the church steps the woman throwing

rice, blond and beautiful, showing no trace
at all of malice in her youthful face.

Now the awful sound, waking me again
like a secret, calls to mind the poison

I left out, and my mother on their bed
tearing a box of letters into shreds.

Tumbleweeds

Rolling nests of the prairie,
prickered and denuded and dead,
clutching at clumps, skipping across
asphalt, whole shrubs ripped out
and flung, and clinging together
like herds racing over acres.
I'd only ever seen them

in Spaghetti Westerns tumbling
quaintly across the painted backdrop—
props blown by big fans and collecting
off-camera against some studio wall.
But here, in Nebraska, they roll
for miles unless a fence catches them.
All day they crunched beneath

my wheels like the delicate skeletons
of small animals. One clutched the grille
and flapped there like a giant bird.
And I felt I could join them, easily,
as stripped as I am, as thin as I've become,
as determined as I am to roll onward.
But even as I dodged them, speeding up

or slowing down, I found myself
feeling satisfied when one met me head-on,
the tread turning branches to chafe.
I relished the champ of their blanched
bodies as my machine ground them to dust,
here where chance seemed perfectly arrayed
and where, once, the deer and antelope played.

A Cold House

I wake now to a house as cold
as your side of our double bed.

Across the threshold, in the dark
hall, the thermostat sparks

a blue star, and downstairs
the boiler thumps like a heart

revived. Hot water shrieks
through pipes till registers tick

like clocks toward a time bearable
and close. I dress in wool

and fleece, keep hands in pockets.
On the couch, our dog looks out

the bay window, his breath
on the glass making a bouquet,

gray flowers which bloom and fade.

Canning Tomatoes

I love the way they slip their skins
and settle into jars,

pink flesh pressed against hot glass
so that I cannot help

but think of sex and the last time
I had it. And their names

vaguely erotic—Early Girl
and Better Boy, Beefsteak

and Sweet. Steam rising from the pot.
Gold bands on the counter

like bangles slid from a thin wrist.
And the round lids' red lips.

Fruit packed in its own murky juice,
and a kind of pact made

at the rim not to leak a word
of it to anyone.

Long after everything has cooled,
some night when I'm eating in,

and thinking of this time I canned them,
the precautions taken

to preserve these bright globes I grew
out of earth, I'll unscrew

counterclockwise and watch them spill
from the jar like a birth.

The Gaze

—*for Betsy*

From the passing plane
we were just one more

wide-awake window
of the many-eyed

colossus, a yellow iris
in the million-visioned

disinterested island.
But had the most

imaginative passenger
ridden our beam of light

he might have seen
for himself that what

shone from your room
was something both old

and new, like the moon
just risen, a trajectory

traced already behind
so many other lit or unlit

windows of the planet
but no less beautiful

for having been done
before. Every pore

of skin on blue skin
a window. Our mouths

windows. Every molecule
of creation a window

and someone or something
on the other side, watching.

Monument

Pink granite moment—
what we went to,
my dog, my God and me

yesterday, yes, today, too,
chasing sticks, sticking
to the road, the south,
and where it went

through Mount Saint Mary's
so as not to desecrate
so as to stay in shade.

Graveyards have
lease laws, not
leash laws,
and besides
I carry a little body bag.

But hold it, the moment—
granite, pink,
when I saw my grandparents' stone,
my dog and me
no longer alone
because my mother
had driven there

—my mother, the survivor,
breast and bladder,
rather not talk about that—

to check on the flowers she'd left,
to touch the last name,
to—I don't know?—show me

the names on the slab's other side,
hers and my father's,
chiseled already,
just the dates
waiting.

A Father's Eyes

My battles ended before they began,
and for that I'm grateful; those neon lips
had too soon kissed the boy from the man,
and hope of truce seemed as absurd as ships
in bottles. But fate sails an unlikely sea.
And gulls flap within the glass. I was saved.
So why do my father's eyes still haunt me
decades later? How to see what they gazed
on the time I crashed in at 4:00 AM?
He didn't speak a word; just stirred the storm
in his cup. But his eyes had grief in them,
and love and recognition. They were warm,
as Priam's might have been to see his boy
dragged by Achilles through the dust of Troy.

Demeter to Persephone

Little whore, little deceiver,
let the rest believe what they will.

You knew enough about fissures,
and that flowers rose

from black ash and flashed
their sex to bees before

they withered. I watched
you sift dust through fingers

and thrust that dirty hand
beneath your linen smalls.

You'd always been enchanted
by talk of shades and souls,

lingering too long at graves,
picking through rotted breasts

of crows for cold keepsakes—
bones for wishes, hearts to range

like stones along a shelf.
I left you seeds, tried my best

to teach the ways of rain
and light. But like the primrose

you opened at night.
Through the crack in the door

I saw you scoop pitch
and smear it, swallow shadows,

paint yourself with soot.
The tines of your hands

had tilled your hot bed
and you were ready to be seeded.

It wasn't ransom I offered
but a handsome dowry—

food for every other mother
and winter for my spite.

Sheep's Skull

I know it is waiting in that storage
garage, wrapped in newspapers in a box,
horned and hollow and bleached by Ireland's
treasured sun. Gaudy bones. An end for books.

She never liked it. The day I carried
it through the cottage door and held it up—
"Alas, poor Yorick!"—she shook her head, said,
"You know you can't take it home, right?" I slipped

it in my suitcase rolled in a sweater.
For four years it gazed through the barrister
bookcase glass in our house, a reminder
of Achill's wasted landscape, our time there,

the hardness beneath our soft flesh. One day
soon I'll retrieve it and my other things.
At times I've thought to give them all away,
start from nothing and see what luck might bring.

But I like those horns, those deep eye sockets,
the passages that once were filled with breath.
I take comfort knowing that I've packed it
again. A keepsake of marriage, life, death.

Double Sonnet

The equivocal eye has come and gone,
gale and rain minced the faith we each depend
upon. Another storm has met its end,
blind to wreckage, utterly overthrown
by its own gyrations. Cities lie prone
as lakes. The sun, as if nothing happened,
strews from its azimuth countless diamonds
on the signed canals, plays like God's trombone
a warm and silent jazz, a *sine qua non*.
Onto half-submerged mansions gulls descend
to vie with anhinga for dividends:
flotsam in the deluge like stepping stones.
And in their tiny, eager eyes is shown
in miniature a scene to apprehend:
what the dove might have had the world been manned
so long and been so ruthlessly outgrown.

Where I tune in, two thousand miles away
in the undestroyed Pacific Northwest,
my hand-crank radio seems strangely apt.
On NPR familiar voices say
what they can to keep listeners abreast,
the general theme being: people adapt.
My own storms seem like showers, a spring day.
I put a fool's trust in the old beau geste,
in time and place. Tomorrow can't be mapped,
unless by miracle or righteous way
we're warned, like Noah, who at God's behest
measured cubits while the thunder clapped.

Transit

Around the world on trains and buses
fuses

real or imagined wait to spark this
darkness

to a brief flash at the speed of an idea.
I hear

what comes before as much as after:
laughter,

cameras clicking, a girl snapping gum,
some

young men discussing football scores,
doors

sighing open or closed, a cell phone's
tones

playing Beethoven's "Moonlight Sonata."
Not a

single seat unoccupied. And maybe
a baby

has started crying and the soothing word
heard

is Arabic or French. Now some other
mother

offers a piece of advice. Streets outside
slide

by like a movie. Even in the bright
light

of day, for every rider the vast, black
back-

of-the-mind reminder that nothing's hum-
drum

now. But we must ride, O God. So we board,
we board.

Autumn in July

All the great shakers are at it again,
or as ever, making news for the world.
Papers have yellowed, their edges have curled,
and those deserts have grown weary of rain.

The end may be near, but here it is just
beginning, again, as ever, with birds
doing what birds do, clouds moving like herds,
and the river announcing what it must.

The leaves have yellowed, their edges have curled,
and, oddly, it is summer still. And ants,
doing what ants do, march through my pantry
carrying spoils back to their little world.

Seven Hummingbirds

at the feeder, peeping for the sweet
water and making wind on my cheek
as I stand among them feeling envious

of their games. They seem so happy
to be dipping, reversing, trading spaces,
clapping one another's wings in mid-air.

They hover inches from my eyes.
Two brush my hand and I understand
I'm there to catch one and hold it,

because I need to, because I know I can.
And it's easier than I would have thought.
Fingers spread beneath the feeder,

just a matter of pressing index to thumb,
and I've got one by the feet, a rufous male,
his back the color of coffee with cream,

a clean splash of orange at the neck,
black legs as thin as a pencil's lead,
and the wings fluttering, stymied,

like a bee at a screen. Cupped in my palm,
his eyes look wild, his feathers ruffled.
His tiny heart quickens my own pulse.

It would take almost no effort to crush
all his bones. This must be how God feels
holding me between calloused time

and the whim of doom. *O tiny, tiny bird!*
But it's the impulse not to squeeze
that I would know. I let it go. I let it go.

Kindling

With a sharp hatchet I shave the ancient
2x8's, pressing the blade and tapping
wood on wood like percussion for a chant

honoring fire. After each long song
I gather into baskets the thin splints,
blow the dust, taste the task upon my tongue.

Once I knew a girl who refused to eat.
She was a ladder I would have climbed rung
for rung. I think I understand her need

now, that beat of ritual, that desire
to splinter at the source of her own heat.
Not unlike my longing to rise higher

with another and lose myself—flash
and burn—at the crux of her mortal fire.
Death in the offing, release. Smoke, flame, ash.

Sapphics on the Rough-Skinned Newt

Toxic swimmers, thousands of them, in my pond,
wiggling black-sperm questions for me as I stand
bent and ready, armed with a net and answers
I wouldn't give them.

Sins of mine—amphibious, star-toed, whip-tailed,
mute transgressions gone unforgiven too long.
Water-borne and treacherous, sedge and dragon-
flies like reminders.

So the net—a Catholic expiation
made of wire and mesh and the need to expose
all my darkest slitherings like penumbras
during eclipses.

Newt on newt. The murky and amoebic water
slick with sex: the jettisoned seed, the poisoned
skin's release, and my uninhibited gaze,
too, like a voyeur's.

Even netted, even in open air they
cling and shine, and something in me would fling them
far but for the deeper desire I have to
swallow each pair whole.

Almost Utopia

If I could cook for her—
    roasted lamb with a demiglace,
        say, or coq au vin

(anything with wine),
    potatoes baked in their dirty skins—
        while her wet clothes

dripped on the line
    and Allen's hummingbirds
        dipped at the sugared water

hung above the deck; and if the light
    was just right, and the breeze
        easy, carrying a dry trace

of bay and the madrones'
    yellow leaves; if she liked
        fresh-ground pepper,

the sound of it cracking
    in the mill, and sea salt, too,
        and coffee sentenced

to the antique oubliette of the hand-
    cranked grinder; our laughter lost
        for a time in the teapot's whistle,

then—what? Who would I be
    for her or for me but the man
        who in the undreamt world

tires too soon of talk
    and can't stand a cluttered table.
        In the middle of some story

told more to fill the empty space
    between our plates than to reveal
        anything meaningful,

I'd find myself dreaming
    of the green river, of the way
        it hugs my legs when I wade in it,

or of the lizard I saw
    doing push-ups on my steps.
        But I'd be looking in her eyes,

wet and brown, and thinking
    at the same time that this
        is what love is—the sweet,

burnt crust of crème brûlée
    and the dark hair that keeps
        falling across her pretty face.

II.

Storm

This is how it happens:
she leaves and once again

they're not speaking.
Something's breaking

and nothing's making sense.
All day the air grows dense,

far-off hills fade in haze,
shrubs loll their tongues

of leaves, and afternoon
shifts from room to room

weighted with waiting.
Not even the cicadas sing.

But in the trees—still, too,
for hours—a pair of blue

jays start to rave. Then a bit
of breeze, as though a jet

has flown by and spewed
in its wide wake a plume

of black. Above their house
the trees now sweep in gusts,

up and down and side to side,
like live wires. And the sky,

long-riled giant, rolls, rolls,
rolls its heavy boulders,

and at the first crack and splash
he runs, he runs to see the flash.

Pit Viper

It comes to me in the night through the grass
of dreams, a living ribbon curled to strike,
guarding some next strange and shifting trespass—

a thing I've done or haven't but would like.
No rattle I recall, no sound at all,
no hissing invitation to its bite.

But a foot will fall where a foot will fall
and might will come what might. Thus the two-pronged
knife, the mind-gall, the choice, the wherewithal

sleep affords the sleeper when all along
he's walked so blindly through his life. A prick
before I see it, like stepping on thorns,

and then the blooming at my feet, the quick,
the chill as if from an open window
in a familiar room, the steady tick

of seconds counted. And they do not slow.
I'm poisoned just by knowing what I know.

The Infidel

A lung, he breathes with wood and arm
    a dark so dark it breaks the moon

and summons up the loon's uncommon
    laughter. Backward and backward, and down

until there's no need to go by sight,
    though mountains loom and what waits

beyond might shatter, he rows
    into her and out of her. He knows

about water, blood, keel and hull,
    the buoyancy of push and pull,

and that there's nothing more than this.
    The body loves itself for what it is.

The Weimaraner

It was a Thursday, you were gone.
It was a summer afternoon, late,
and I craved the cool and easy

of a movie, people in a foreign land,
people with problems like mine
but who had gods and scripts

and two hours to solve them.
When the light turned green,
I heard it—a squeal, a screech,

the sound wheels make like no other.
And at first I thought it was me,
that I'd accelerated too quickly,

that my bald tires had spun
because the pavement was still wet
from the rain, which had come

through like an army and left—
everything charged and dripping.
And you were gone and I was alone

but for my dog, who when I left him
wanted to come and stood at the gate
beseechingly. Steam on the pavement,

the smell of burnt rubber, a brown car
pulled over, something blue-gray
against the sidewalk and trying to rise.

Across the street the Lutheran church
with its closed eyes, its red door locked.
The thing rose and fell and rose,

its neck long, its snout dripping blood,
and it was too big and it was still daylight
so it couldn't have been a possum.

It fell and tried to rise. Two boys
emerged from the brown car. I stopped.
"It ran out of nowhere," one said.

"I didn't even see it," said the other.
Brothers, maybe. And me, and the thing
struggling in its going, broken

and in pain. And I wanted to tell you
right away. A small crowd gathered.
A brunette girl with a blanket. A thin man

with a phone. Then my quiet ride
on the winding mountain road,
the sun falling into the hills,

the theater almost empty,
cool and almost empty. A movie
about a couple in Italy, their problems,

their desires, their lives so easy to fix.
You were gone but I was there
and then home with my dog,

who greeted me with paws and tongue
and wide eyes. And I held him—
for all the barrenness near and far,

for all that was broken, for all who were gone
or there, I held his warm, panting body.
Without God, without words but with

all the time in the world, I held him.

Total Lunar Eclipse

The night the planet's shadow
slid across the moon and made
an eye, I'd left the sliding door
wide open, and that was how
the wind snuck in, why the flame
winked, why the candle wept
down one mauve side. What more
was there? The Sox were up one
run in the final Series game.
Trick-or-treaters caterwauled
along the hill. A lone doe stepped
like an apparition through the trees.
You were facing east-bound
in a breakdown lane, or so you said,
and through our invisible connection,
I could hear the whoosh of eighteen-
wheelers percuss your risible,
forced story of campaigning
for Kerry in the Keystone State.
My hens squawked once and went
quiet. The sky was a black page,
the moon a closed parenthesis,
then an open. I heard the Sox score
another run, saw the black river
brighten. I was the same old me.
But you were someone new
out there in the pines, on a freeway,
in your yellow Mini, moving now,
smoking again (I could hear that, too),
third gear, then fourth, revving,
speeding, and I was on our deck
bundled up for the eclipse.

Fear of Flying

Even then, without knowing it, I saw that everything
was blue. Far off, I sensed some endless falling —
by dint of remembrance, the curve of a star calling
me back. My father loaded me into the small plane.
My mother waved from the paved deck, her kerchief
in the airport's breeze puffed up like a windsock.
There were more dials on the panel than a shop of clocks.
When the door clicked shut, my father gave a brief
salute and cranked a lever so the propeller whirred.
Passenger and pilot, we sped until the wheels spun
on nothing, until nothing but science kept us in the air.
My mother was a dot below us. Or vision had blurred.
Or else I see her that way, through the lens of a plane
on an hour's ride, just to bring my father back to her.

Wren in the House

Some time during the day,
in the afternoon as I imagine it,
while I was stuck in school

moving from room to room
when the bells told me to,
full of purpose and plans

and the thought of divorce
as cool as the silver band
resting on my nightstand,

the winter wren, lured by
some vague need, must have
squeezed through a slit

in the screen, or snuck in
when the red door blew open,
or else followed Gus

through his flap like a second pet.
On the way home, caught
in traffic again, I watched

the other drivers mouthing
words into headsets, bobbing
to music, applying lipstick—

all of them strapped in
and, like me, trapped in lives
like little windowed rooms.

But the wren. By then
it must have tired itself out
flying from screen to screen,

resting on a dusty blade
of the ceiling fan, peeping
its story to the shifting day.

When I found it there,
shivering, weak, barely able
to fly, it was more than

I could have hoped for—
its white, darting eyes;
its sharp claws wrapped

like a ring around my finger;
its body soft and warm
and ready to be revived

beneath the heavy sky.

The Experiment

Late in the day, way after the last bell's rung
and the choir has tired of its well-learned songs,
and all the teachers have gone home, but one,
he sometimes wanders into the science wing
to dream the dream of an old concoction:
two parts love to one part time—the reaction,
warm as a Bunsen burner, that somehow joined
that positively charged pair. So amazing
how their eyes first met, how they'd go on seeing
those same strange changes day after day,
and if only he could teach that in English Lit,
make all of them understand they're good at it.

ʊ

First Year Teacher to His Students

Go now into summer, into the backs of cars,
into the black maws of your own changing,
onto the boardwalks of a thousand splinters,
onto the beaches of a hundred fond memories
in wait, where the sea in all its indefatigability
stammers at the invitation. Go to your vacation,

to the late morning cool of your basement rooms,
the honeysuckle evening of the first kiss, the first
dip and pivot, swivel and twist. Go to where
the clipper ships sail far upriver, where the salmon
swim in the clean, cool pools just to spawn.
Wake to what the spider unspools into a silver

dawn dripping with light. Sleep in sleeping bags,
sleep in sand, sleep at someone else's house
in a land you've never been, where the dreamers
dream in a language you only half understand.
Slip beneath the sheets, slide toward the plate,
swing beneath the bandstand where the secret

things await. Be glad, or be sad if you want,
but be, and be a part of all that marches past
like a parade, and wade through it or swim in it
or dive in it with your eyes open and your mind
open to wind, rain, long days of sun and longer
nights of city lights mixing on wet streets like paint.

Stay up so late that you forget day-of-the-week,
week-of-the-month, month-of-the-year of what
might be the best summer, the summer
best remembered by the scar, or by the taste
you'll never now forget of someone's lips,
and the trips you took—there, there, there,

where snow still slept atop some alpine peak,
or where the moon rose so low you could see
its tranquil seas…and all your life it'll be like
some familiar body that stayed with you one night,
one summer, one year, when you were young,
and how everywhere you walked, it followed.

God in the Machine

How quietly it happens, the way a mushroom
opens under damp leaves. Suddenly it's there
and you don't know it, not even a whisper,
not even a rumor of bad news, a pea forgotten

in a pocket. My mother's grew in her bladder,
a colony of bumps, like air bubbles clinging
to the inside of a glass. My grandmother's
hid in her breast. My father's in the thin skin

of his brow, a blotch he might have mistaken
for a rash. Today I spoke with my friend Jim.
His has ravaged his pancreas and his liver.
He manages now in morphine's twilight dream.

What trespasses, what unforgiven sins that the body
should turn so treacherous? Sorcery of cells,
bedevilment of blood, and the brain as useless as bells
without clappers. Where's the cure? Where's the God we

believed in? Indiscriminate plague: some get saved,
some don't. And should it sweeten my every breath
to still breathe, when there's so much death,
so many acres awaiting graves?

The Artist

Frost, crows, stillness.
This house, its ghost,
the hour I love most,
when through cold glass

I watch no one pass,
and dawn draw gold
the lines of one old
colonial. Here, at this

desk, I will solve no
great calamity, produce
nothing at all of use
to humanity, show

no artistry as lovely
as that sunlit porch.
I will merely watch.
Frost fades. Crows fly by.

Here comes the first car.
How am I different
from that indifferent
and blameless star?

Pawtucket, Rhode Island: An
Interment

Once upon a time it must have been quaint—
old Slater's place the only industry,
the rest rolling pasture and willow-tree
banks along the Blackstone. No chipped-paint

tenements, no I-95. The bricks
of mills still red clay waiting to be fired—
like the millions who would live and die here.
I see the waterwheels turn like clocks.

I hear the huge looms rattle, the spindles
spin thread down to dowels, the stone-on-stone
knock of building. And dirt flung where the bones
of my ancestors lie. We light candles

in the chapel for our final goodbyes.
Outside a wet snow falls into rows
of graves. The past begins and ends right now,
here where grief powers the machines of my eyes.

Ovens

"I see the killer in him
and he turns on an oven,
an oven, an oven, an oven...."
        —*Anne Sexton*

Hot boxes, wire-tiered
and dark, slow-glow
electric or four blue
cities of flames on top,

and names like Amana
and Sharp. Most of them
windowed thick, Cyclopic,
mastermind with a master

plot, and something always
a little off of ON or OFF
—the dial nudged, the hiss
of gas, a clock that forgets

to speak up. Mostly the jaw
drops with a breath of heat
to deliver the leg of lamb,
the roast of beef—all juicy

and hot. But sometimes
it does not. A crock cracks,
a casserole bleeds out,
Easy-Off poisons the house.

A cockroach cooks. Or a mouse.
There was Plath in her flat
on Primrose Hill with her poems
and her pills and her doubt.

And years before that, all over
Poland the terrible smell
and the cough. God, God,
God, turn the dial to Off.

Prayer

Out of the mouth of brain,
because more is a must,
and up from dust
and centuries,

we demand the deaf one
listen, or else we talk
like a wall clock
forgotten

in a move, in a room full
of sunlight through
which a single
fruit fly passes.

Memento Mori

Poland, Rwanda, Sudan...

He digs because it's the job he's given,
and he does it in the dark reckoning
all the ways it's just. Soon the sickening
will be dressed and the blisters forgiven

by his hands. The spade's blade will dry, the field
heal without a scar. Now there is no why,
just the work itself: the moon like an eye
watching, the tool helping the earth to yield,

a mosquito insisting at his ear.
He disregards the contents of the cart,
but it wants attention: blue twisted parts,
like a basket of crabs, staining the air.

He digs only as deep as he needs to,
tips the cart, kicks the spilled limbs. But the hole
is never deep enough. Though it settles
it'll rise again—Darfurian, Tutsi, Jew....

The Colors of Things

I.

They probably didn't intend to hang us, those projects
boys, all dark-skinned-shirtless, filthy, sour, and stuck in
the hate of late afternoon. When they came upon us
with our hank of rope, the woods shushed us, a daytime
moon blinked its pale eye above their fused silhouette.
Peripherally, a sun-blazed leaf waved crazily. Up close,
they were body odor, biceps, a gold tooth. You want the
truth? When they knotted the noose I pissed myself.
When they tied us at the waist, ass on ass, I felt the spin
cycle of our meshed terror, felt the wetness spread. For
a second I saw the worst—both of us one dead
pendulum. Things spiraled in the black holes of the
biggest boy's tired eyes, escape velocity at the speed of
light. They closed, opened. Then he laughed. Hard. So
hard I swear I saw tears.

II.

The fall before the spring we separated. My wife and I,
in the yard. Morning split-wood sharp, our last chance
before the killing frost. Fifty tulips, variegated, their
little white beards of roots. Rocky soil, a garden shovel's
bent blade. A pared apple we shared. Our dog burying
a bone. I wonder what they looked like, those tulips. If
the new owners cut some for a vase. I've always put too
much hope in the colors of things.

Beating a Dusty Rug

This rug remembers, wears the evidence,
the number of times I've left or entered.
Its threads are woven now with pounded-
down pieces of my past—the West's red
clay; the Bread Belt's black loam specks;
the East's ground-up shells, my home turf.
It holds the days I drank and days I didn't.
This pine needle—did I carry that back
from the walk I took after I quit my job?
Or did I pick it up in the backyard taking
a banana peel out to the compost heap?
This rug's braids also keep the dander
of my dead cats, flecks of their shit and litter;
the mingled pubic hair of my married life,
the skin cells we shed, the fingernails
and toenails, eyelashes and scabs and snot.
Peat from Ireland; Pompeii's volcanic dust;
coral sands of Anguilla, St. Croix, St. John;
a blade of grass carried home from Stonehenge.
Mud from a garden. Feather from a coop.
Blood and coffee and fabric and glue.
I, too, cleave to my past and abrade.
Really, this rug is a tapestry of my time,
each day a spindle on a loom. So out of
what rage or regret or need for expiation
do I beat it with the handle of a broom?

Bellevue, Paris, New York, Wherever

A boy falls from a window or a roof,
no feathers, no wax, the sun hardly out,
the peace of dinner broken by a shout.
Flies and neighbors gather demanding proof.

The cat in 14-B blinks from its sill.
But where is the boy's mother? His father—
don't you know?—was killed last year in the war;
she took a second job to pay the bills.

A siren navigates the labyrinth
of streets until its red lights dance across
the body covered now with sheets. The loss
deepens in the hush. When the ambulance

rolls away (no rush now), people shake heads
and cough, spent but reluctant to unfold
their arms and ascend the stairs to their cold
plates, their evening news, their familiar beds.

But there is the mother to consider—
how, later, she saw the blood-stained pavement,
and by the open window comprehended
the weight of that falling as it hit her.

Falmouth

Weeks that summer we fled the house
on the island where our grandfather
was dying, and kept to the estuary,

netting blue claws in green currents,
digging for clams in the black mud.
Weeks that summer fled. The house,

when the tide turned and riverbanks
bequeathed their small dull treasures,
was a dying place, so we kept the estuary

secret and gathered our fear like
netting blue claws in the green currents.
Weak but fed on summer and the house

full of children, my grandfather came out
when the tide turned. Along riverbanks
where drying crabs crept up the estuary

to die in the sun, we dragged his catamaran
and gathered like our secret fears
that week of summer when he fled the house,
and his dying swept us like the estuary.

The Poem Speaks (for Itself)

"But what do I really inhabit to inherit?"
— Claudia Rankine

These bones hold no envy old enough to
know

better. The marrow—narrow passages—
presages

an emptying to be filled with symbols'
symbols,

letters jockeying to become, like platelets,
clots

in the blood of the new and never-lasting
thing

called poem.
                        This one's about my father's twice-
sliced

carotids, brain-feeding couplets, pipes
scraped

clean as the briarwoods he reamed with resin-
stained

toothpicks and wires. He lived to tell about
it—

the pain, the little apoplexy, his tongue's
strange

palsy that made *say* become *they,* and *dinner*
thinner.

He told me then he wanted to write
but

didn't know a participle from a gerund,
and

as he talked he struggled to make *worths*
into *words.*

I said, *Me, too.* It was sweet how he wanted to be
me,

to inhabit the creature he'd
made.

Water, Father, an Unsteady Boat

He and I cut an awkward, crisscrossed wedge,
a wake of whorls gurgling back to black glass,
and in the rear I could hardly see him
for the fog. His paddle knocked at the prow,

its blade dripping, our silence like a pledge
of truce to our ancient war of redress.
I owed him as much, as far as we'd come
through the portage of years and our somehow

still burdensome need to push from the edge
into the deeper mystery of us.
Perhaps this was why he taught me to swim,
for the passage he couldn't help but allow:

water, father, an unsteady boat, the ledge
toward which we rush, buoyant and yet hapless,
where lakes become rivers, rivers become
seas in the confluence of then and now.

Rubaiyat for Chanterelles

I wait for them the way I might
a lover. Visited at night
by visions soft and golden—flesh
of cap and slit of gill—I fight

my sleep to step instead through trees.
No doubt like love it's a disease
of mind and body—wide and deep,
its roots as mycelial as these

October fruits'—this need to find
and lose oneself at once in blind
pursuit. The hunt's the thing that feeds:
the forest damp and cool with vines

as sweet as shampooed hair; the oaks
all smooth and posed in their baroque
undress; a kind of eagerness
in that autumnal air, like smoke

before a fire. I wander thus
the edge of sleep a man obsessed
with love—the fungus rarely found
and only sometimes poisonous.

Jays Raving at Dawn

Once again I'm ratcheted
    out of darkness and into dim vision:
        the cabin cold and damp as a grave.

The jays, the jays, the jays.
    Same web between glass and screen.
        Like me it has changed little

these many days. It trembles,
    vacant silk, like the scarf of a baby's
        ghost, and despite this being

the first thing I see when I wake,
    I like this time the most. Stretching
        my toes into the cool space a wife

once occupied in that life
    that seems sometimes like a dream.
        The jays. The clicking of claws

on the floor when my dog
    and I rise together. Water filling
        the empty heart of the kettle. Blue

flames. The tiny brown
    mountain of coffee dressing
        the pantry with its smell. And the jays,

the jays. I can see them now
    through the kitchen window,
        a family of them, blue and proud.

The jays, the jays, the jays.

Conch

Between the rolling sheets of low-tide foam
    I find it—this prize I've tried for
        all week.

No crab claw, as first I thought, but a bone-
    white tube, like paper curled,
        and when I pull

it's as though the sand pulls back. I pluck it,
    a giant tooth from the mouth
        of the beach,

tip it like an urn and a drab grout weeps
    from the orange spout.
        Now it's a trumpet

clogged with a flat black foot, rough as fine-grit,
    and gray meat which when I touch it
        puckers lewdly.

I know she'll love it, will smile when I take it
    from behind my back, this living
        offering.

I know I will have to kill it, too. Already
    I'm imagining the *clickclickclick*,
        the blue tongues,

the pot and the water and the silent scream
    that is part of the taking
        requisite to giving.

Don't we each wrench the wild out of the other,
    if only to hold up to the light
        our own base origins?

When I pry out the animal it will drop in the sink
    with a sloppy thud, and we'll have
        the empty shell,

the potential music. Later, we'll soak it in a bucket
    of bleach, scrub it clean for the bookcase
        or the mantelpiece.

Tomorrow I'll wade in the surf searching
    for another. To make a pair.
        One for each of us.

Gary J. Whitehead has previously published one full-length collection, *The Velocity of Dust* (Salmon, 2004), and three chapbooks of poetry. He has been the recipient of a New York Foundation for the Arts Fellowship in Poetry, the Pearl Hogrefe Fellowship in Creative Writing at Iowa State University, and the PEN Northwest Margery Davis Boyden Wilderness Writing Residency. An oil painter and crossword constructor as well as a poet, he lives in the Hudson Valley of New York and teaches English at Tenafly High School in New Jersey.

CPSIA information can be obtained at www.ICGtesting.com
Printed in the USA
268605BV00001B/78/P